Date: 10/4/13

J 945 TIE
Tieck, Sarah,
Italy /

ITALY

EXPLORE THE COUNTRIES

Sarah Tieck

Big Buddy BOOKS
Explore the Countries

VISIT US AT
www.abdopublishing.com

Published by ABDO Publishing Company, PO Box 398166, Minneapolis, MN 55439.

Printed in the United States of America, North Mankato, Minnesota.
052013
092013

 PRINTED ON RECYCLED PAPER

Coordinating Series Editor: Rochelle Baltzer
Contributing Editors: Megan M. Gunderson, Marcia Zappa
Graphic Design: Adam Craven
Cover Photograph: *Shutterstock*: Rechitan Sorin.
Interior Photographs/Illustrations: *AP Photo*: Antonio Calanni (p. 11), Kike Calvo via AP Images (p. 31), North Wind Picture Archives via AP Images (pp. 13, 33), L'Osservatore Romano (p. 33), Markus Schreiber, File (p. 19), The Yomiuri Shimbun via AP Images (p. 25); *Getty Images*: Apic (p. 17), Carlo Lasinio (p. 31), Martin Moos (p. 35), Suzanne Plunkett/Bloomberg via Getty Images (p. 15); *Glow Images*: Joerg Reuther (p. 23); *Shutterstock*: Kosarev Alexander (p. 25), andras_csontos (p. 21), cesc_assawin (p. 29), Claudio Giovanni Colombo (p. 23), deepblue-photographer (p. 35), Claudio Divizia (p. 35), elen_studio (p. 11), Globe Turner (pp. 19, 38), Robert Hoetink (p. 37), JeniFoto (pp. 5, 34), Viacheslav Lopatin (p. 9), Robyn Mackenzie (p. 27), Pecold (p. 34), Bill Perry (p. 16), Maryna Pleshkun (p. 38).

Country population and area figures taken from the CIA World Factbook.

Library of Congress Control Number: 2013932153

Cataloging-in-Publication Data

Tieck, Sarah.
 Italy / Sarah Tieck.
  p. cm. -- (Explore the countries)
ISBN 978-1-61783-814-9 (lib. bdg.)
1. Italy--Juvenile literature. I. Title.
945--dc23
                                                        2013932153

Contents

Around the World

Our world has many countries. Each country has beautiful land. It has its own rich history. And, the people have their own languages and ways of life.

Italy is a country in Europe. What do you know about Italy? Let's learn more about this place and its story!

Did You Know?

Italian is the official language of Italy.

Italy has many coastal cities.

Passport to Italy

Italy is a country in southern Europe. Four countries border it. The Mediterranean Sea is to the east, south, and west. Sardinia and Sicily are islands of Italy.

Italy's total area is 116,348 square miles (301,340 sq km). More than 61 million people live there.

6

WHERE IN THE WORLD?

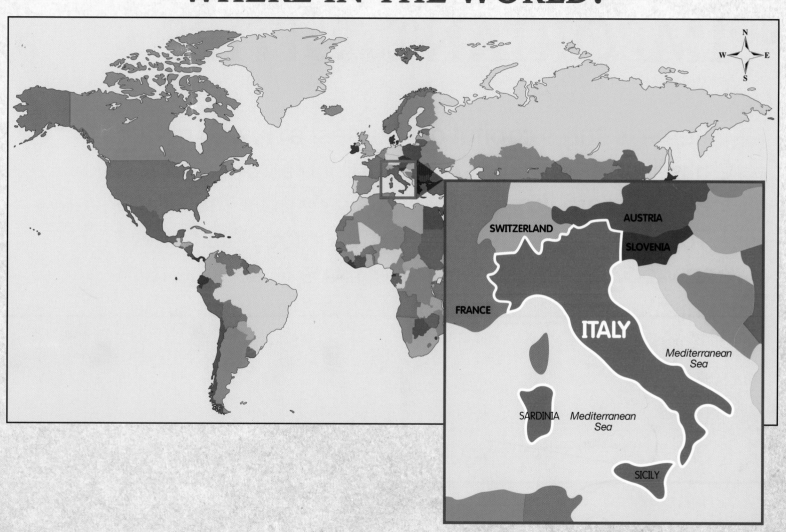

SWITZERLAND

AUSTRIA

SLOVENIA

FRANCE

ITALY

Mediterranean Sea

SARDINIA

Mediterranean Sea

SICILY

IMPORTANT CITIES

Rome is Italy's **capital** and largest city, with about 2.6 million people. It is known for its history. Rome was founded more than 2,000 years ago near the Tiber River.

Today, Rome is home to many famous buildings and works of art. Visitors travel there to see the ruins of historic buildings. One of the most popular is the Colosseum.

SAY IT

Colosseum
kah-luh-SEE-uhm

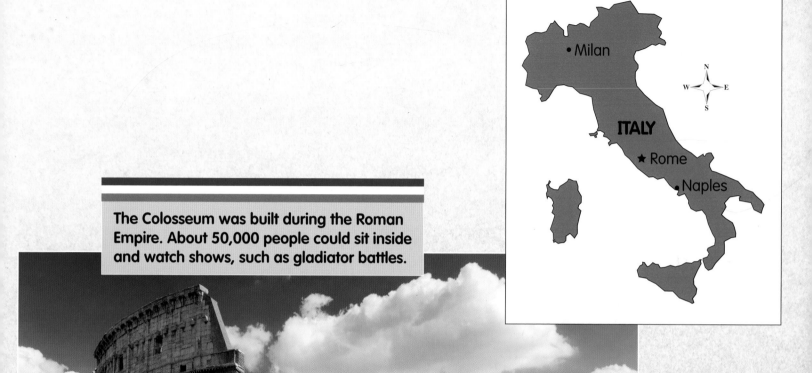

The Colosseum was built during the Roman Empire. About 50,000 people could sit inside and watch shows, such as gladiator battles.

Milan is Italy's second-largest city. It is home to about 1.2 million people. Located near the Alps, Milan is a center for business and trade. Many visitors come to see its ancient buildings and important works of art.

Naples is Italy's third-largest city, with more than 960,000 people. This hilly city is on Italy's west coast. Mount Vesuvius is about seven miles (11 km) from the city. This famous **volcano** is still active.

The *Last Supper* is a famous painting in Milan. Leonardo da Vinci painted it in about 1497.

Naples has one of Italy's key ports.

Italy in History

The Roman **Empire** was based in what is now Italy. The city of Rome was founded in 753 BC. It became the heart of the Roman Empire.

The Roman Empire began in 27 BC. It ruled parts of Europe, the Middle East, and Africa.

Over time, the empire grew too big to be controlled from Rome. It split apart for good in AD 395. For many years afterward, different groups fought to control the land.

Ancient Rome was famous for its power and way of life.

When the Roman Empire was strongest,
it included more than 50 million people.

In the 1300s, a movement called the Renaissance began in Italy. This was a time of learning, ideas, and growth in the arts. Famous paintings, buildings, inventions, and sculptures were created.

Over the years, different parts of Italy were controlled by different rulers. In 1870, they came together as one country. Around 1922, Benito Mussolini became the country's leader. He believed in **fascism**.

In 1940, Italy entered **World War II** on Germany's side. In 1943, it gave up and joined the fight against Germany. Two years later, Mussolini was killed. In 1946, Italy became a **republic**.

Did You Know?

Mussolini took control of businesses, newspapers, police, and schools.

Lorenzo de' Medici was a ruler of Florence, Italy, in the 1400s. He was known for supporting the arts.

Timeline

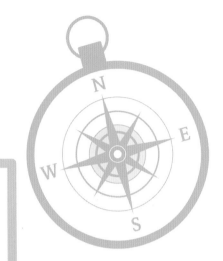

About 1298

Famous Italian explorer Marco Polo completed his book *Description of the World*. It was about his travels to Asia. Many people were excited by his stories!

476

The western part of the Roman **Empire** broke apart. The eastern part became the Byzantine Empire.

1436

The dome of the cathedral of Florence was completed. Filippo Brunelleschi came up with the way to build it. This was an important discovery.

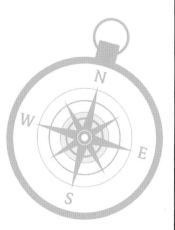

1796

Napoleon I of France invaded Italy for the first time. He wouldn't be completely defeated until 1815.

2013

In March, Pope Francis became the new leader of the Roman Catholic Church. As the pope, he lives in Vatican City.

About 1503

Leonardo da Vinci began painting the *Mona Lisa*.

An Important Symbol

Italy's flag was first used in 1796. It has green, white, and red stripes. It was based on France's flag. But, it used the colors of Milan.

Italy's government is a **republic**. Its parliament makes laws. There are two houses. They are the Chamber of Deputies and the Senate. The president is the head of state. The prime minister is the head of government.

Italy's current flag was officially adopted in 1946.

Italy's parliament chose Giorgio Napolitano as president in 2013.

ACROSS THE LAND

Italy has mountains, coasts, forests, islands, **volcanoes**, and grassy areas. The Po Valley, or Northern Italian Plain, has rich farmland. The Alps and Apennines are large mountain ranges.

The country is shaped like a boot. It is surrounded by the Mediterranean Sea on three sides. Major rivers include the Po and the Tiber.

The island of Sicily is home to Mount Etna. This is one of Europe's largest active volcanoes.

Did You Know?

In January, the average temperature in Rome is 45°F (7°C). In July, it is 78°F (26°C).

Many types of animals make their homes in Italy. These include wolves, wild boars, and deer. Birds such as vultures, buzzards, and falcons also live in Italy.

Italy's land is home to many different plants. These include oak, beech, cypress, and olive trees. Heather and water lilies grow there, too.

Wild boars and pigs are common in Italy's national parks.

Cypress trees have wood that is known for its strong smell.

EARNING A LIVING

Italy makes many products. Cars, leather, and shoes are made there. Some people work in the country's factories. Others have service jobs in business. Many work for hotels or restaurants.

Italy has important natural **resources**. Natural gas and pumice come from the country's land. Farmers produce grapes, olives, apricots, and artichokes. They raise cattle, hogs, sheep, and chickens.

Italy is known for fashion. Gucci is one famous Italian fashion designer.

Ferrari sports cars are made in Italy.

Life in Italy

Italy is a modern country. It is known for its beauty, history, and art. Many well-known artists, writers, and thinkers have come from this country.

Italy is also famous for its food. Different parts of Italy have different ways of cooking. Favorite Italian foods include pasta, pizza, cheese, and risotto. Veal, pork, and fish are often found in Italian dishes.

Did You Know?

In Italy, children must attend school from ages 6 to about 16.

Antipasto is often the first course of an Italian meal. It includes cold meats and vegetables.

Italians love football, or soccer. Many cities have teams, and people play for fun in parks. Basketball is also popular. Other favorite activities are fishing, roller-skating, baseball, biking, and watching movies.

Religion is important in Italy. Most Italians are Roman Catholic. Vatican City is in Rome but is not ruled by Italy. It is the center for the Roman Catholic Church.

FAMOUS FACES

Many talented artists are from Italy. Leonardo da Vinci was known for his paintings and his ideas in science. He was born in central Italy on April 15, 1452.

Leonardo liked to learn how things worked. He knew about plants, human bodies, the earth, the stars, math, and other subjects. He is famous for paintings such as the *Mona Lisa* and *The Last Supper*.

SAY IT

Leonardo da Vinci
lee-uh-NAHR-doh duh VIHN-chee

The *Mona Lisa* is famous for her smile.

Leonardo kept notebooks full of his ideas and drawings.

Michelangelo was another famous Italian artist. He was born in Caprese on March 6, 1475.

Michelangelo made sculptures, paintings, and **architecture**. In 1504, he finished the *David*. This sculpture showed the famous king from Israel.

In 1512, he finished painting the ceiling of the Sistine Chapel in Vatican City. He also designed buildings before his death in 1564.

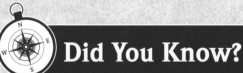

Did You Know?

People once thought Michelangelo painted the ceiling while lying on his back. He actually painted it standing up! He wrote funny poems about his neck hurting and paint dripping in his eyes.

Between 1508 and 1512, Michelangelo painted the ceiling of the Sistine Chapel. He mixed paint with wet plaster. This is called fresco. He had to work quickly before it dried.

Michelangelo was known for making many pieces of art. Sometimes he left projects unfinished.

Tour Book

Have you ever been to Italy? If you visit the country, here are some places to go and things to do!

 ## Remember

Visit the ancient ruins of the city of Pompeii. It was destroyed when Mount Vesuvius erupted in AD 79. The ruins show how people lived almost 2,000 years ago!

 ## Explore

See Venice. This famous port city is actually a group of islands. People don't drive cars. Instead, they ride in boats such as gondolas.

 Listen

See an opera at the Teatro alla Scala opera house in Milan.

 Learn

Visit the city of Florence. There you can see artists making leather products, jewelry, and pottery.

 Discover

Have a slice of pizza in Naples. It was invented there! Today, the city is still famous for its pizza.

A GREAT COUNTRY

The story of Italy is important to our world. The people and places that make up this country offer something special. They help make the world a more beautiful, interesting place.

Building started on the Leaning Tower of Pisa in 1173 in Pisa. This bell tower is famous because it leans to one side.

37

Italy Up Close

Official Name: Repubblica Italiana (Italian Republic)

Flag:

Population (rank): 61,261,254 (July 2012 est.) (23rd most-populated country)

Total Area (rank): 116,348 square miles (72nd largest country)

Capital: Rome

Official Language: Italian

Currency: Euro

Form of Government: Republic

National Anthem: "Fratelli d'Italia" (Brothers of Italy)

Important Words

architecture (AHR-kuh-tehk-chuhr) the art or science of building.

capital a city where government leaders meet.

empire a large group of states or countries under one ruler called an emperor or empress.

fascism (FA-shih-zuhm) a movement that values nation and race above individuals. A fascist government has a ruler who controls many parts of people's lives.

republic a government that has a leader who is usually a president, not a king or queen.

resource a supply of something useful or valued.

volcano a deep opening in Earth's surface from which hot liquid rock or steam comes out.

World War II a war fought in Europe, Asia, and Africa from 1939 to 1945.

Web Sites

To learn more about Italy, visit ABDO Publishing Company online. Web sites about Italy are featured on our Book Links page. These links are routinely monitored and updated to provide the most current information available.

www.abdopublishing.com

Index